YOU HAVE THE FINAL SAY IN MATTERS OF YOUR LIFE

You Have the Final Say in Matters of Your Life

N Esquire

Copyright © 2025 by Naldine Philistin
All rights reserved. No part of this book may be reproduced in any manner whatsoever without written permission except in the case of brief quotations embodied in critical articles and reviews. The contents of this book are based on the ideas of the author and are not to be construed as legal or professional advice.
First Printing, 2025

ISBN 979-8-218-75960-5

To the people who think they can't create their desired outcomes, you can. Honoring yourself is always a win in my casebook.

Preface

I may not know you personally, but if you feel drawn to read this book, we're now connected. This book is a testimony that you're a creator and have everything you need to thrive. I felt compelled to name my book, "You Have the Final Say in Matters of Your Life," to affirm that in the case of you versus any situation, you win.

With that said, I know that my book will empower you. While I may use "you" throughout the book, I'm also speaking and affirming myself. My intention is to create a written source for myself while being an example to you of how I win in matters of my life. The rest is up to you.

The design is also by intention. In law school, my casebooks were dense, heavy and expensive. Carrying cases felt like a burden. Therefore, my book is lightweight and the perfect size to carry with you. The content is also easy to digest.

Every case starts with a background. So, let's start with my case.

Legal Background

I thought I wanted to be a lawyer because people told me that role would suit me. In hindsight, I didn't know myself to choose the best career fit.

After playing the role of *Esquire*, I stepped back from practicing law and accepted a nonlegal counselor role. The break from fighting people's battles felt like a relief. What seemed to be a professional setback led to my personal growth. I no longer thought that people needed me to advocate for them. I knew that people held the power to stand in their truth and create their desired outcomes. So, I repurposed my lawyering skills and taught people how to "practice" advocating for themselves.

Today, I still "practice," but I only take on *my* cases. The truth is, you don't become an advocate until you start practicing and the best person to start with is you. No one is more qualified than you to get your desired outcomes.

So here are the relevant lessons I took away from law school and how I apply them to my life now.

N Esquire

Contents

Dedication   v
Preface   vii
Legal Background   ix

   I Prerequisites to Practicing   1
  II Solo Practitioner: CRACk Your Cases   6
 III Your "Just in Case" Backup Team   14
 IV Advocating for Parties of a Case   16
  V Final Brief: Honor Yourself   17

Summary   19
Practice CRACking Your Case   20
Acknowledgments   21

I

Prerequisites to Practicing

In my state, law school is a prerequisite to practice as an attorney. There, you study rules, cases and how to think like a lawyer. Law professors also stress that ignorance of the law isn't an excuse!

You spend a majority of your life in school studying core subjects, except for the most important one. To start practicing on *your* matters, ignorance of yourself isn't an excuse either.

Do both. Study other subjects (people included) and yourself. Self-awareness is a prerequisite to practicing self-advocacy.

Continuing Education

In my case, I had a Juris Doctor (JD) degree but was uneducated on self. Had I done the inner work then, I'd skip law school and the six-figure debt (that's now paid off). Since I can't change my past choices, I'm taking a new course and continuing my education on self.

The burden was on me to ask who am I without the attorney status and title? What do I like or dislike? What are my desires and triggers?

Questioning yourself is part of your continuing education and the answers are within you. You're the primary source and don't need to spend over your means on tuition and books. Your life is the case study.

Once you question yourself and find the answers, you question everything outside of you. Your self-awareness changes how you perceive situations. Your mind expands.

For example, there are no right or wrong answers in law school. The answer is, "It depends." Infinite outcomes exist depending on how you apply the rules to the facts of a case. Life is the same. Situations aren't black and white. In fact, multiple truths exist at the same time. So, your perception matters.

I also mastered my analytical, reading and communication skills. Now, I think for myself before agreeing with others' beliefs. I read my body and energy, which are guides in navigating my life. I speak up for myself in everyday matters.

It's worth noting that your continuing education is a lifelong process. There's no graduation or degree at the end of your studies. The reward is self-mastery.

Creating Your Rules & Code of Conduct

By the time you graduate law school and sit for the bar exam, you know hundreds of rules of law and exceptions. Rules establish order and control. They require your participation and agreement to apply to you. However, most people unconsciously follow rules without question. Before law school, I was a law-abiding follower.

This is why your continuing education is worth it. You become an exception to the rule. Self-mastered people question the status quo. They create and live by their own rules and code of conduct. They're in control and hold themselves to high standards. They make conscious choices and achieve desired outcomes. They're self-governing and accountable for their thoughts and actions. They know there's no one to appeal to but themselves. They have the final say in matters of their lives.

So be exceptional, not the general rule. Create your own rules and code of conduct while having a general knowledge of the rules that govern everyone.

Getting Your License to Practice

After you pass your state's bar exam, you generally can't hold yourself out as an attorney and represent clients until you satisfy additional requirements and are deemed fit to practice law. Otherwise, you may be engaging in the unauthorized practice of law.

In your life, you're the licensing authority and don't need permission from anyone to advocate for yourself. Once you study yourself and feel ready to start "practicing," you give yourself a license or permission to practice. No one is more fit than you to advocate on your behalf.

So, use your license to practice self-advocacy now.

II

Solo Practitioner: CRACk Your Cases

The real advocacy starts outside of the classroom. Law school and bar exams are easy compared to real life matters because they happen within controlled settings. The stakes are higher in your life. Failing an exam isn't as disappointing as losing in life. So when you start practicing, trial and error are part of your work.

Whether you're prepared or not, life situations happen at any time. Your response determines if you win or lose your cases. Be proactive now to prevent situations from manifesting into serious issues in the future.

And it's ok to make mistakes or lose your trials. When you're tried or tested, the power rests with you to end the test or trial whenever you want. As a solo practitioner, I call it the case of, "Don't Try Me Again." Learn from your losses and win the next case.

To date, I have a 100% success rate in *my* cases. Partly because I'm my only client. I have more time and energy to invest in myself than I did as an attorney. And I've been practicing self-advocacy for years.

To win my cases, I follow a decision-making process that's inspired by law school. Infinite possibilities exist to win your cases, and you're not bound to follow my method.

The Consultation: Think About Your Matter

When situations arise, sit down and consult with yourself. Bring the facts and supporting materials to your table for review. Take time to think about the matter. Then, take your own advice and make the best decision for you.

At times, you may decide to consult with a trusted person about your matter. You may consider outside advice. However, defer the "Final Say" to you.

CRAC v. IRAC

There are two methods that law schools teach their students to structure their legal writing and arguments. CRAC stands for conclusion, rule, application, and conclusion. IRAC stands for issue, rule, application, and conclusion.

In my practice, I CRAC my cases. I like CRAC because when you focus solely on spotting issues under the IRAC method, that's all you see. You become an issue-spotter, which may cause you to make everything in your life an issue.

CRAC leads you to think outside of issues by starting and ending with a conclusion. You get to choose not to make a situation an issue and make the best decision for you.

So, let me break down my version of the CRAC method.

CRAC Revised

Conclusion: When situations arise, decide that you don't have a problem. Ask yourself (*Your Honor*) what you want the desired outcome to be. Then, make a decision that aligns with your desires. When you *honor yourself*, you win, even if external circumstances appear otherwise.

Rule: You're the ruler in your life. You hold the power to create rules, change them or make exceptions. You have the only and final say in matters about you. You may consider outside rules, but they don't trump yours. If you consider outside rules, you do so strategically because they bolster your decision.

Application: Take action steps towards your decision. Make a *motion*.

Conclusion: Uphold your decision and trust your *judgment*.

Award: Celebrate the win of honoring yourself.

After you follow the revised CRAC method, rest your case because you know you won. It's impossible to lose when you honor yourself. There's no need to argue back and forth like you're in litigation. Save yourself the burnout and fatigue. There's no one to appeal your final decision to but you. So, you win.

Let's practice CRACking a case.

CRACking a Case Example

Facts: Your boss asks you to do something that would compromise your integrity and code of conduct. You feel uncomfortable with the request.

On its face, this situation seems problematic. Instead of looking at it as a problem, see it as an opportunity to exercise your power of choice and honor yourself, which is a guaranteed win in my book.

So, let's CRACk this case.

First, think about the matter and trust how you feel. If your boss puts you on the spot or creates a sense of urgency, take your time to respond. You may state to your boss, "I need to think about your request."

Here, you're not accusing your boss of any wrongdoing or making an uninformed decision out of fear or pressure. You're making it clear that you make conscious choices. Trust yourself to know when something feels unaligned with you. The more you practice honoring yourself, the more comfortable you feel.

Conclusion: I honor myself and can't perform my boss's request.

Rule: I will not engage in any activities that compromise my integrity and personal rules of conduct.

*You may consider outside resources such as your employee handbook, ethical rules for professional conduct and applicable laws, if they support your decision.

Application: Speak to my boss immediately and respectfully decline the request.

Conclusion: I'm not obligated to honor my boss's request if it conflicts with my rules and code of conduct.

Award: Treat myself to lunch for honoring myself.

To manage your expectations, there may be consequences to declining your boss's request. Yet you still win because you honored yourself. If your boss takes adverse action against you, CRACk your case and consider alternative options. Or perhaps, your boss may respect your decision and think twice about the requests they make. Your "No" may prevent future issues and reset workplace boundaries. Whatever the outcome, focus on yourself.

III

Your "Just in Case" Backup Team

There are cases where seeking help may be necessary and in your best interests. It's important to have a backup team or resource list of professionals for "Just in Case" situations. Therefore, you may work with an attorney or nonlegal advocate to handle your matters. No matter who you work with, vet your backup team members and remember that you have the final say in your matters. If you give away your decision-making power to third parties, you lose.

For people to be part of my backup team, my admission standards are high. From my experience, people who dishonor themselves are likely to dishonor you. So, I'm selective about who I work with and perform my due diligence of assessing a third party's character and fitness. They also must have experience advocating for themselves and getting favorable outcomes. I use outside resources to leverage success, not to lose my cases.

Choose your backup team wisely to leverage success in your life too.

IV

Advocating for Parties of a Case

Not everyone desires or has the capacity to handle their own affairs. Therefore, they may need an advocate. Once you do the self-work, you decide if pursuing a legal career or advocacy in a nonlegal capacity is the best fit for you. Advocating for others may be your life's calling and you should honor that call.

If you take away anything from my case, practice now! To be the best advocate for other parties, you need to start with you. You don't need a degree or license to handle your everyday matters. If you can think, read and communicate, you can CRACk situations like an *Esquire* before they get out of hand and require legal intervention.

And if you think that you can't handle your own matters, think again. When you reframe your thoughts, you unlock a door to infinite possibilities.

V

Final Brief: Honor Yourself

B efore I close my case, let me share a final thought. Throughout my life, the tests and choices I made worked out in my favor and led to the creation of this book. I didn't pass the tests alone. I must acknowledge the special parties who had my back and "prepped" me to win my cases.

My parents were my primary examples of self-advocacy and they never went to law school. I witnessed them successfully defend themselves in situations and make choices to create the best life for our family. They prepared me for the real tests in life.

As a first year law student "1L," I recall the thought and consideration I received from the upper Ls. Because of them, I didn't start law school from scratch. They shared their class notes (aka "outlines") and exam prep tips, which helped me survive the law school curve. My fellow Ls were also my study partners and we got through law school and the bar exam together.

Post-bar, I passed three rounds of interviews and accepted a job offer at a private firm where the partners and senior attorneys mentored me. They briefed me on everything I needed to know to succeed as an *Esquire* and protect myself from professional liability.

While practicing, I studied other people's cases to mitigate (to the extent possible) any unfavorable outcomes in my life. My clients prepared me on how to overcome life hardships.

Now, I get to pass my case notes to you. May you win your cases too.

When in doubt, just *honor yourself* (emphasis added).

Summary

Step 1: When situations arise, control your perception. Instead of looking at situations as problems, see them as opportunities to honor yourself.

Step 2: Sit down with yourself for a consultation and think about the matter. You may consider the advice or opinion of a neutral, third party. However, you have the final say.

Step 3: Bring the facts and supporting materials to your table for review.

Step 4: CRACk your case like *N Esquire* or follow your own decision-making process.

Step 5: Award yourself for choosing yourself. You deserve it.

Practice CRACking Your Case

Facts:

Conclusion:

Rule:

Application:

Conclusion:

Award:

Acknowledgments

I am eternally grateful for my...

Creator who gives me everything I need to live in abundance.

Mom, dad and stepdad who love me and invested in my growth and success since birth.

Sister who sprinkled her creative magic on me.

Siblings who inspire me to be a trailblazer.

Friends and family, who have my back, always.

Fellow Esquires, law professors, and former bosses and clients who taught me to be the best advocate.

I honor you all.

www.ingramcontent.com/pod-product-compliance
Lightning Source LLC
Chambersburg PA
CBHW020243010526
44107CB00002B/73